Getting Past the Pain Between Us

Healing and Reconciliation
Without Compromise

A Nonviolent Communication^{SM}
presentation and workshop transcription by

Marshall B. Rosenberg, Ph.D.

PuddleDancer
P R E S S

P.O. Box 231129, Encinitas, CA 92023-1129
email@PuddleDancer.com • www.PuddleDancer.com

For additional information:
Center for Nonviolent Communication, 2428 Foothill Blvd., Suite E, La Crescenta, CA 91214
Tel: 818-957-9393 • Fax: 818-957-1424 • E-mail: cnvc@CNVC.org • Website: www.CNVC.org

ISBN: 1-892005-07-7

Contents

Getting Past the Pain

Introduction

The following was excerpted from a workshop given on October 4, 2002 by Marshall Rosenberg, founder of the Center for Nonviolent Communication. *Getting Past the Pain* focuses on mending our relationships with each other and gives us skills for understanding and resolving our conflicts, for healing old hurts, and for developing satisfying relationships using Nonviolent Communication℠ (NVC).

Here you will find steps you can take for the healing or reconciliation of any conflicted relationship, whether at work, at home, at school, or in your community. It will also give you a sense of the energy of empathy: the compassion and the heartfelt "presence" necessary for healing to take place. Nonviolent Communication skills empower you to make lasting peace, and even to prevent trouble from happening in the first place. Join in on this workshop dialogue and enjoy the magic that understanding brings when we listen and speak from the heart.

The training opens with Marshall Rosenberg role-playing a situation posed by an audience member. In the role plays, participants are identified as UF (unidentified female participant), UM (unidentified male participant), and MBR (Marshall B. Rosenberg). All other words are Marshall's. We pick up the conversation with a question from one of the participants of the workshop.

Role-Play: Healing Bitterness

MBR: Good afternoon. So, what could I share with you about healing and reconciliation that would meet your needs? Would you like to hear me talk about it? Or maybe you have some pain left over from something that happened to you in the past with somebody, and would like us to do it "live" and not just talk about it?

UF: I wonder how I can get past or release a lot of bitterness I have towards somebody.

MBR: How about if I use Nonviolent Communication and play the role of the person that you have the bitterness towards? I'll be that person, but I'm going to be speaking to you as someone living Nonviolent Communication. All you need to do is just say what you want to say. Okay, you got the game? Good, now who am I going to be?

UF: My brother.

MBR: (BEGINS PLAYING THE ROLE) Sister, I am very touched that you want to heal this bitterness between us, and by the courage you're showing. What would be a big gift to me is if you would share what is alive with you right now in relationship to me. Just say what's going on however you want to.

UF: I have a real ethical problem with you. You weren't honest with me or reliable when our parents were declining. When I reached out to you to try and work it out, you were unwilling. You just wanted to put the past behind us. That's what you've always done, our whole life. You say it's my problem; you don't want to deal with it. Whatever is upsetting to me doesn't seem to matter.

MBR: You've said a lot to me here, a lot of different feelings: Let me check to be sure I understand fully. I'm hearing a lot of anger connecting to a need you may have had for more support when our parents were declining. Did I hear that much right?

UF: Yes.

MBR: So that was real, and you'd like some understanding now about how difficult this was for you to go through, how you would've really loved support . . . but not only didn't you get that support that you would've liked, but I'm also hearing that some of the things that I did since then in relationship to family matters have left you with a great deal of pain . . . that you would have really liked us to have made those decisions differently . . .

UF: Yeah.

MBR: Yeah . . . especially since it wasn't the only time you've experienced that your own needs weren't given the consideration you would've liked. Did I hear your message accurately?

UF: Yeah, yeah.

MBR: Do you like me when I'm wearing empathy ears?

UF: Yes! Will you be my brother?

MBR: So, still wearing these ears, I'd like to hear whatever else is still alive, still going on in you.

UF: You say you want us to get back together, but I just can't. We just don't resolve conflicts in the family, and I don't want to live like that any more.

MBR: So, if I hear your need, it's to protect yourself from the pain that you've felt in the past when you've reached out and tried to resolve things and it didn't happen. At this point you've had enough of that. It's as if part of you would like to hear from me, but not if it means going through the pain that you've felt in the past.

UF: Right. I'm still left in a quandary, because I can't see it working either way. If I go back, it's not going to be good for me, but then just staying away seems unnatural.

MBR: So, you're really torn. You have two needs. One need is for there to be reconciliation and healing between us. The other is this strong need to protect yourself. You don't know how to meet both needs.

UF: Right.

MBR: That's a real painful conflict.

UF: Right.

MBR: Anything else, Sister, that you'd like me to hear before I react to what you've said?

UF: No.

MBR: Hearing you now, with these empathy ears on, I feel a deep,

deep sadness, because I can see that I have not met my own needs with some of the things that I've done in our relationship: my need to nurture you in the way that I'd like, to contribute to your well-being. When I see how my actions have just the opposite effect, how it's created so much pain for you, I feel a deep sadness . . . and I'm very vulnerable right now . . . I'd like to hear how you feel when I tell you about this sadness.

UF: You're probably in the same quandary that I am, in the sense that you don't know how to meet my needs without being highly uncomfortable yourself . . .

MBR: I want to thank you for anticipating that, and what I'd really like right now is for you to just hear how sad I feel that I didn't get my need met to contribute to your well being as I would've liked.

UF: I appreciate that.

MBR: Now, what I would like to do is tell you what was going on in me when I did those things in our relationship. And—I think you've already somewhat anticipated this—I'd like to make it as clear as I can. First, about not providing more support for your efforts in dealing with the stress around our parents when they were declining: I had an inner message telling me that I really should help, and that I was a rat for not giving more support. And then because I was feeling so guilty, I wasn't able to hear your pain and your needs with my compassionate listening ears. Your requests were sounding too much like a demand on me. I was torn because I wanted to help, but I was also angry hearing a demand. I felt guilty, and I just didn't know how to handle all of those feelings going on in me except to try to avoid the whole issue. I'd like to know how you feel when I tell you that.

UF: It makes sense . . . clarifies things.

MBR: So then, just as you have some hurt in relationship to me, I have some hurt that I haven't known how to express to you about things that have happened in the past. I wish I could've known how to talk about it, but having that hurt inside and not knowing how to express it made it come out angry towards you at times. I wish I could have expressed it differently. So, how do you feel when I tell you that?

UF: Good to hear.

MBR: So, is there anything else that you'd like me to hear or you want to say, or that you want to hear from me?

UF: I guess I'd want to know how to work through this in a way that is comfortable enough for each of us. Then we can move forward. It's a mess that has to be cleaned up. And I'm willing to hear whatever you have to say, to open the dialogue.

MBR: (Still role playing) I have an idea. Tell me how this feels to you: How about asking the folks who are recording this workshop to send me a copy of this as a start? And then maybe call me and ask me if I'd like to continue this kind of dialogue, maybe with the help of a third party?

UF: Yeah, I think that's an excellent idea.

MBR: Okay, let's do it. (END OF ROLE PLAY)

UF: Thank you.

Reactions to the Role-Play

MBR: Okay, any reactions to that situation? Questions?

UF: What would you recommend in the event that sending the tape was not a possibility?

MBR: I think we got some of the healing accomplished that she wanted, that we dealt with the hurt. She wants to deepen the relationship. That shows that we don't have to have the other person physically available to get some healing. Sure, it would be nice now to deepen things with him and go further, but we don't want to depend on the other person's availability for our own healing to take place. Especially if they're not alive any more, if they're inaccessible. Fortunately we can heal *fully* without the other person being involved.

UM: It seems to me to be very important, if I have an issue with a person that I cannot heal by myself, to have somebody who is able to play the NVC part with me. Like you did right now, someone who is able to listen to my issues and listen empathically. So my question is, if I don't have that friend, do you have a method to do that with myself?

MBR: Yes, I think you can do it with yourself, and certainly in the best of all worlds, we would have had the brother here. That would have been even more powerful. He could have played himself. But we can do it without him.

Let me outline the steps we went through to help do that. What's very important is to notice how little we talked about the past. Sister made very brief reference to what I, the brother, did, but we didn't go into detail. And what I've found over the years is the more we talk about the past, the less we heal from it. Most of our conversation was about what was alive in both of us right now. We were talking about the present, what she's still feeling as a result of what happened in the past.

Most people think you have to understand the past to get healing. And that you have to tell the story to get the understanding. They mix up intellectual understanding with empathy. Empathy is where the healing comes from. Telling the story does give intellectual understanding about why the person did it, but that's not empathy, and it doesn't do any healing. In fact, retelling the story deepens the pain. It's like reliving the pain again. So, while we're not denying the past, and we make reference to it—to what the brother did—we didn't go into the details. We didn't say, for example, "I had to take Mother to all the stores and not only that, but when Dad got sick, you know, dadadadadadada." The more she would've talked about that, the less healing would've happened. Especially when you do it with the people you have pain about. They're not going to see that your objective is to get understanding for the pain. They're going to think your objective is to create a case to send them to hell.

UF: I was kind of getting this feeling that the brother has issues that he hasn't expressed to her around this: What if he's holding stuff against her?

MBR: As the brother, at the end I said, "I'm feeling some hurt that I don't know how to express to you." That's all I need to do. I said that I was still feeling some hurt in relationship to the past for which I need some understanding, and that understanding doesn't mean that I have to tell the story, to talk more about the past.

UF: Right.

MBR: It just means I got it back from her. I saw in her eyes that she heard it.

UF: Okay, okay.

The First Two Steps in Healing: What's Alive Now and Empathic Connection

MBR: So, the **first step** in healing, whether we want to heal ourselves or help somebody else to heal, is to put the *focus on what's alive now*, not what happened in the past. If there is a discussion of the past, say five words, no more: when you ran away from home, when you hit me, whatever.

Our **second step** is to deal with what's alive in us now in relationship to that. The next thing that I'd like you to keep in mind from that first situation, in my role of the brother, is that I *empathically connected* to what is alive in her now. Doing that requires certain things.

The first component to empathic connection is what Martin Buber calls the most precious gift one human being can give to another: presence. In the role of the brother I was fully present to what was alive in her now, in this moment. I wasn't thinking of what I was going to say next, or what happened in the past.

This is a hard gift to give to somebody because it means that I can bring nothing in from the past. Even a diagnosis I've had of this person in the past will get in the way of empathy. This is why my clinical training in psychoanalysis was a deficit. It taught me how to sit and think about what the person was saying and how to intellectually interpret it, but not how to be fully present to this person (which is really where the healing comes from). To be fully present I have to throw out all of my clinical training, all of my diagnoses, all of this prior knowledge about human beings and their development. That only gives me intellectual understanding, which blocks empathy.

The best I can tell you about what empathy feels like to me is that it's like surfboard riding. You're trying to get with the energy of the wave, trying to hear what's alive right now. I'm trying to go with this rhythm of life that's in this person. And sometimes just looking at the floor I can get more with it than looking at the person and being distracted by things.

UF: I get sucked into sympathy, though.

Empathy versus Sympathy

MBR: Sympathy, empathy—let's get clear about the difference. If I have strong feelings in me, just being conscious of them is sympathy, not empathy. So, if I had been the brother and I had said, "Boy, I feel sad when you say that," that would have been sympathy, not empathy. Remember a time when you had a pain in your body, maybe a headache or a toothache, and you got into a good book? What happened to the pain? You weren't aware of it. It was there, I mean the physical condition hadn't changed, but you weren't home. You were out visiting: That's empathy. You were visiting the book.

With empathy, we're with the other person. That doesn't mean we feel their feelings. We're with them while they are feeling their feelings. Now, if I take my mind away from the person for one second, I may notice I have strong feelings. If so, I don't try to push my feelings down. I say, "Go back to them." My own feelings tell me I'm not with the other person. I'm home again. "Go back."

If my pain is too great, I can't empathize. So I can say, "I'm in so much pain right now hearing some things you've said—I'm not able to listen. Could we give me a few moments to deal with that so that I can go back to hearing you?"

It's important not to mix up empathy and sympathy, because when this person is in pain and then I say, "Oh, I understand how you feel and I feel so sad about that," I take the flow away from them, bring their attention over to me.

I sometimes use a phrase that many people hate about Nonviolent Communication, and say that it requires "learning how to enjoy another person's pain." Now, why do I use such a sick phrase? Because when I would come to San Diego, a friend of mine would call me on the phone and say, "Come over and play with my pain." She knew that I knew what she meant by that. She was dying of a very painful disease and she used to tell me that what made it even worse was having to deal with other people's reaction to her pain. Their response coming out of their good sympathetic hearts was creating so much of a problem for her that she would rather be alone with her pain than to have to end up taking care of other people around it. And so, she said, "That's why I like to call you, Marshall, because you're so cold hearted. You're such a miserable son-of-a-bitch. I know I can talk with you and you're not going to give a damn about anybody but yourself."

She knew I could understand "idiomatic NVC." And she knew that I considered it a pleasure in the sense that whether the other person is experiencing pain or joy, when we are present to them in a certain way, it's precious. Of course, I would rather the person be experiencing joy, but it's precious just to be there with another person and with whatever is alive in them. That's what my friend meant by "play with my pain."

UM: How do you stay really present and not get swept up in all these feelings?

Staying Present in the Face of Strong Feelings

MBR: I don't know how to do that all the time. I was trying to do some healing work with a woman from Algeria, who wanted some healing from me. Extremists had dragged her outside and made her watch while they tied her best friend behind a car and dragged this friend to her death. Then they took her inside and raped her in front of her parents. They were going to come back the next night and kill her, but she got to a phone and called friends of mine in Geneva who got her out in the middle of the night.

I got a phone call from them where I live in Switzerland. And they said, "Marshall, can you do the healing work with this woman?" They told me what had happened. I said, "I'm doing a training during the day, but send her over this evening." They said, "Marshall, here's the problem. We told her how you'll do the healing work, that you will play the role of the other person: She's afraid she'll kill you." I said, "You explained this is role-play, it's not the actual person?" They said, "She understands that. But she says, 'Even if I imagine he's that person, I'll kill him, I know I will.' And, Marshall, you should know that she's a large woman."

I thanked them for the warning, and then I said, "I'll tell you what. I'm going to have to have an interpreter in the room. It might make her feel safer to know that there's going to be another person there. I got a guy in my training from Rwanda and after what he's been through, I don't think this will scare him. Ask her if she would feel safe if this guy from Rwanda is in there to help me out if I need help." So those were the conditions under which she was there.

Now, to address your question: When I started to hear this woman's pain, the enormity of her suffering, twice I just said, "Time out, time out. I need time." I had to go out into the hall and do a lot of work on myself to be able to go back. I couldn't just "go back" to her. The only thing I wanted to do at that point is find that guy and do a little "Detroit therapy" with him. I had to work on myself for twenty minutes or so before I could go back to her.

What I'm saying, then, is that sometimes my pain is so great I'm not able to be as fully present as I'd like. And I haven't found that to be a big problem. The other person can understand it usually.

UM: Marshall, don't you think it's helpful sometimes to share that pain with the other person?

MBR: Very often I do. I say to the other person, "I'm in such pain I can't hear you right now. Do you want to hear what that is, or are you in too much pain?" I'd say half the time they want to hear it and they can. So that's another option. In this case though, she was crying so hard and screaming, I wasn't at all optimistic that she needed to deal with my feelings.

UM: That's very helpful.

Empathy Steps

MBR: Back to our empathy steps. **First,** empathy requires presence, a focus on what is alive in the other person at this moment, on their feelings and needs. **Second,** it requires checking things out with the other person, making sure you're connecting with their feelings and needs.

Each step we've mentioned so far can be done silently: being fully present, having your attention on the other person's feelings and needs. Or, we could check it out verbally, reflect out loud what we sense the feelings and needs are.

Let's also remember to have our intention be on creating empathy, as opposed to practicing a mechanical technique. The number one reason is to be sure we're connecting to this person. We don't want the other person to see us as using something on them. So when we check it out, we do it in a way that lets them know we're not sure we're connecting fully and we'd like to verify what's real for them about that.

The other condition under which we might check it out— even if we're pretty confident we've heard them—occurs when we sense that they really made themselves vulnerable in saying what they did. We can guess, if we were in that position, that we would really appreciate some confirmation that we were understood. So if we picked that up and guessed it, to then say it out loud to check it out. These are the only two conditions under which we communicate empathy out loud instead of silently.

MBR: I was recently in Denmark working with a woman with an enormous amount of pain. At least twenty minutes had passed. She really expressed her pain very beautifully, but she did it pretty nakedly. It was very easy for me to hear what was alive in her. I didn't feel any need to reflect it out loud, so for twenty minutes I sat there silently. At the end of those twenty minutes she just jumped up and hugged me and said, "Thank you for all of that empathy, Marshall." I had not said one word. I was with her the whole time. She felt it without a word being spoken.

UF: So, with empathy, you're empty of yourself and full of the other person.

MBR: With empathy, I'm fully *with* them, not full of them—that's sympathy.

Giving Empathy Back

The **third** step for empathizing is to stay with the person until they give you signs that they're finished. Be aware that very often the first one or two messages that people give us are but the tip of the iceberg: We haven't gotten down to the bottom. There are a couple of signs to help us tell whether the person is finished with the empathy. One sign is the relief you can feel in them: Empathy feels damn good, so if that person got the empathy they need, you can feel that sense of relief, and you'll feel it in your own body. Anyone in the room with you will feel it. Another sign is they will often stop talking.

The **fourth** step doesn't happen until the relief is felt. During the empathy process, if every time I understand something and they come back with, "Yes, and blablablablablabla," that's a signal that they need more empathy. But when I feel this relief in tension, when I see that the person has stopped talking, chances are they've had the empathy they've needed. But I always like to triple check by saying to them, "Is there more that you'd like to say?" I've learned to be very slow in shifting my attention away from the other person to myself. It doesn't hurt to check again.

It would help if the person we are doing the empathy work with knew how to say, "Finished," but most people don't. And most of the time, even after the empathy, they want something else. Our **fifth** step, then, is to empathize with their "post-empathic" request, that something extra they want. That might be information about how we feel having heard what they've said, especially if they've been very vulnerable.

It's a very human thing to want to know how what you've given has affected the other person. Still, most people don't know how to ask for that. So if, after the empathy, I see them looking at me, I usually say, "Would you like to hear how I feel about what you said?" Sometimes they do, and sometimes they don't want to hear how I feel.

Besides wanting information about how the person giving empathy feels, sometimes the post-empathic request is for some kind of advice about better meeting their needs. When it comes to advising your child, however, never give advice unless you receive a request in writing first signed by a lawyer. Triple check that they want advice, because it's almost always my first reaction to skip the empathy and go directly to the advice.

Empathy Review

MBR: Having outlined the steps for the post-empathic request, let's look again at our role-playing situation, and bring up another question you may have about it.

We started with me playing the role of the other person—the brother—giving the sister empathy for her pain. Being with her, I sensed that she would like to get some verification, and I asked out loud most of the time. I tried to be fully present to her feelings and needs. Now, notice I did that in the role of the brother: Why didn't I do it just as myself? I think that *anyone* giving her empathy would have worked to help heal her.

However, over the years, I've found that it's more powerful the closer it comes to the real thing. In our example here, if the brother was around, I would've wanted to help him give that empathy directly to his sister. But since she didn't have him here today, I played the role of the brother.

To sum up, then, the first step in the healing process is to get someone the empathy they need. There are three ways to do it: You can give it as a third party, you can play the role of the other person involved, or get that other person there to give it in person.

Mourning in NVC

MBR: The second overall step in the healing process is "mourning." In the role of the brother, after the empathy, I mourned. Here's what that sounded like: "Sister, when I see how my actions have contributed to your pain, I feel very sad. It didn't meet my need to nurture and support you in a way I really would've liked."

The main thing here is that it requires that we see a big difference between mourning and apology. I see apology as a very violent act. It is violent to the person receiving it and violent to the person giving it. And what's even more tragic is the person receiving it usually likes it, addicted by the culture to want the person to suffer and see them hating themselves. What I find to be true is that nobody will ever apologize or want an apology if they have experienced sincere mourning instead.

Let's look at the difference between mourning and apology more closely. Apology is based on moralistic judgment, that what I did was wrong and I should suffer for it, even hate myself for what I did. That's radically different than mourning, which is not based on moralistic judgments. Mourning is based on life-serving judgments. Did I meet my own needs? No. Then what need didn't I meet?

When we are in touch with our unmet need we never feel shame, guilt, self-anger, or the depression that we feel when we think that what we did was wrong. We feel sadness, deep sadness, sometimes frustration, but never depression, guilt, anger, or shame. Those four feelings tell us we are making moralistic judgments at the moment we are feelings those feelings. Anger, depression, guilt, and shame are the product of the thinking that is at the base of violence on our planet. And I'm glad to have those feelings, because if I'm thinking in a way that I believe supports violence on our planet, I want to as quickly as possible transform that thinking.

In our second step, then, I mourned; I didn't apologize, I mourned.

Getting Unstuck

UF: In your work do you come across people that go into mourning and don't find a way to complete it?

MBR: No, usually what keeps us stuck is moralistic thinking and judgments. I like the way Ernest Becker, the anthropologist, puts it in his book *Revolution in Psychiatry.* He agrees with Thomas Szasz, a psychiatrist, that "mental illness" is a tragic metaphor. He shows a different way of looking at the phenomenon. Becker's definition of depression relates to your idea about getting stuck and never coming out of it: "Depression results from cognitively arrested alternatives." What he means by that is that our thinking blocks us from being aware of our needs, and then being able to take action to meet our needs.

Let's take an example of someone mourning that is having trouble completing. If the person mourning thinks over and over, "I'm a poor parent. If I had treated my child differently, he wouldn't have run away from home and been killed on the train, running away from me . . . I should've known better, what's wrong with me, I'm a terrible parent . . ." You get the idea. That can go on for years and years and the person never gets out of it. But that's not mourning. That's getting stuck in moralistic thinking, all the "should haves." That doesn't go anywhere. "I'm a terrible person," is static thinking. That's what gets us stuck.

UF: Could you repeat that quotation and explain a little more about it?

MBR: "Depression results from cognitively arrested alternatives." Translated in my language, it's that our thinking keeps us from being aware of our needs (and taking steps to meet our needs). We get stuck in our thoughts.

I'll give another example. I work with very depressed people labeled as "bi-polar" this and "depressive reaction" that. They sit there so depressed, thinking, "Oh, I don't want to live." If I use the empathic language of Nonviolent Communication and ask, "Could you tell me what needs of yours are not getting met?" I would get from them, "I'm a terrible failure." I'm asking their needs, but they're telling me what they as people are: "I'm a terrible friend."

MBR: We also get stuck if we compare ourselves to someone else: "My sister's two years younger than me, and she's an administrator in her business. Look at me. I'm only an assistant supervisor." I'm stuck by comparing.

If you're comparing yourself to others, you must have read Dan Greenberg's book *How to Make Yourself Miserable.* One chapter teaches that, if you don't know how to be depressed, just compare yourself to other people. And if you don't know how to do that, he's got some exercises. One shows a picture of a man and a woman who would be described as handsome, beautiful by contemporary standards. All of their measurements are on the picture. Greenberg's exercise is this: Take your measurements, compare them to these beautiful people, and think about the difference. You can start off happy, and I guarantee if you do that exercise, you're going to end up depressed.

Greenberg doesn't stop there. Just when you thought you were as depressed as you can get, you turn the page and he says, "Now, this is just a warm up, because we all know that beauty is skin deep and that's not important. Let's now compare ourselves to people on dimensions that are important. Like what have you achieved in your stage of life with some other people that I have pulled at random from the phone book. I've interviewed these people and asked them what they've achieved, and now you can compare yourself. So, the first person he gets out of the phone book is Mozart. I don't know a lot about history, but I don't think Mozart had a phone, so I don't entirely trust Greenberg here, but anyway, he says this man, Mozart, has written several pieces of music which have lasted over the centuries as masterpieces, et cetera, et cetera.

UF: Started when he was five.

MBR: Started when he was five. Now compare what you've achieved at your stage in life with what Mozart had achieved by age five. You can see that comparing yourself to others doesn't get you anywhere. That can go on forever; you never get out of it. That kind of thinking is taught in the schools, supported by the manufacturers of anti-depressants. The more you think that way, the more business is going to be good.

Healing Review

MBR: Let's briefly review the steps we've taken. First, Sister got empathy from me in the role of Brother. Second, I, the brother, mourned—not apologized, mourned—and that required a consciousness of my needs that weren't met. Third, I expressed the feelings that came with those needs not getting met.

In the next, or fourth, stage of the healing process, we turn the empathy role around and we have the sister empathize with what was going on in the brother when he did what he did. So playing the role of the brother I said to her, "I'd really like to tell you what was going on in me at the time that I was doing that. I had these messages inside my head telling me I should help you, hearing them coming from outside of me. Understand Sister, that I'm not saying you yourself said those messages, but I was hearing them inside of me, and as a demand. So I was torn inside: I wanted to help you, and at the same time, my need for autonomy was threatened by my hearing 'shoulds' inside and outside."

In this stage in our healing process—of getting empathy for

the person who did the act that stimulated the other person's pain—it's very important that it be done when the person in pain is ready to empathize. Almost always, people who have been in a lot of pain tell me that they've had somebody say, "You should empathize with the other person. If you empathize you'll feel better about it." It's true I think that the healing is deep when we can empathize with what's going on in the person who raped us, who did something harmful to us. But to ask people to do that before they have had the empathy they need first is just to commit further violence to them.

As a further example, let's go back to that woman that I mentioned earlier from Algeria and to the part of the process where I was going to play the role of the other person expressing what was going on in me (him) when I (he) violated her so terribly. Twice she had screamed at me, "How could you have done it?" She was asking me, "How," because there is a hunger in people to understand. But each time she said it, I could see she was still in too much pain herself to listen and give me empathy.

I'm very slow to get to this fourth step of the whole process; I want to make sure the other person has had the empathy they need first. So, I said, "I will tell you, but first I want to be sure that you've got all the understanding you need." When that is finished, the woman, any person, is usually hungry to empathize with me, with the other person who has hurt them.

UM: I was experimenting with NVC once, with somebody else also practicing. What really upsets me is that when I am trying to do it, the other person also practicing empathy, says, "Okay, you didn't express your feelings," or, "You didn't . . ." Maybe practicing has to be a little mechanical in the beginning, but can't the technique be more of a natural process? If I skip a step, I want to have freedom to do that. For example, you said that after empathy, you mourn. If I'm so structure oriented that I think I need to do everything exactly literally, then if I don't feel like mourning, I will be fake with myself, which is exactly the opposite of what I think it is you're suggesting to be in contact with. I really have a need to remind myself that the technique is a great help, but won't work for me by itself without being true to what I'm feeling in that moment.

Process versus Mechanics

MBR: I like very much what you're saying. It was said in a little different way by a woman in Zurich, Switzerland. She came to a workshop and saw a husband and wife working with me, and what happened when they empathically connected with each other in a conflict that they'd had for a long time. She saw how beautiful it was to just see the energy in their faces when for once they weren't having enemy images, and were really hearing each other. And it had been a very painful conflict, maybe fifteen years of going over it.

The Swiss woman comes back a year later and she says, "You know, Marshall, in the year since I was in your workshop, every time I'm in a difficult situation I bring to my consciousness the look on the woman's and man's face when they connected empathically," and then she says, "then even when I speak in a hurtful or harming way, it's still NVC."

You see, she had it the way you do now. The mechanics are only helpful to the degree to which they support our connecting in a certain way. If we get so preoccupied with the mechanics that they become the only objective, we've lost the process.

Now, this is one of the hardest things about our training because one of the things that people say they like about our training is that it really helps them manifest in concrete ways what they've always believed. So, they like the fact that it is a way of concretely manifesting, but its very concreteness can be a disadvantage when it becomes an objective to do it right.

Slowing Down and Taking Time

UF: I'm working and struggling in my life with this whole issue of slowing my body down, slowing my relationships down so I can be more present to myself and to other people and to life. I see you doing this constant traveling. I would find it inspiring and helpful to hear if it's true that you weren't always this slow, and little bit about the evolution of how you slowed yourself down.

MBR: And I think it's related to what he's (Male participant, above) saying, because it's in the middle of that rat race that it's very important for me to know how to choose to make use of these three words which I probably said to myself more than any three words in the last forty years: "TAKE YOUR TIME." Those three words give you the power to come from a spirituality of your own choosing, not the one you were programmed for.

In my meditation materials, I have a very powerful picture that helps me to remember to take my time. A friend of mine from Israel is very active organizing Israelis and Palestinians who've lost children in the struggle, and who want to create something else out of the misery. So, one of the steps was to write a book in honor of his son who was killed, using the energy that he suffered from that to go in a different direction. He gave me a copy of it and even though it was written in Hebrew and I couldn't read it, I am glad he did, because I opened it up and there on the first page is the last picture taken of his son before he was killed in the battle of Lebanon. On the son's T-shirt it says, "Take Your Time."

I asked my friend, the author father, if he had a bigger-sized picture that I could have to help me remember. I told him why those three words were so important to me. He said, "Then let me tell you also, Marshall, this will probably make it even more powerful. When I went to my son's commanding officer to ask, 'Why did you send him? Couldn't you see that anybody you asked to do that was going to get killed?' he said, 'We didn't take our time.' That's why I put that picture in there of my son."

It's critical for me to be able to slow down, take my time, to come from an energy I choose, the one I believe that we were meant to come from, not the one I was programmed into.

My Israeli friend also said, "Marshall, I'll give you a poem written by an Israeli poet who was influenced the same way you were when he saw the picture." And the first line in his poem is, "Take your time, it's yours you know." And I have to keep working at that because as my beloved partner keeps pointing out, I forget it and I start to race.

Empathy for Those Who Would Hurt You

UF: I've heard you say that children are less likely to be beaten by someone if they empathize with the person ready to beat them. I assume this applies to adults as well. Do you have any suggestions or emergency phrases that they might pull out at that time?

MBR: Yes. The first thing we teach them is never to put your "but" in your dad's face when he's angry. So, when Daddy says, "Why did you do this?" don't reply, "But, Dad." Never give an explanation. What to do instead is, as fast as you can, put your attention on what this person is feeling and needing. Be conscious that they're not angry at you, you didn't make them angry. But hear their anger and hear what need isn't getting met.

We practice, practice, practice this. It's one thing to talk about that theoretically, but it's another thing when someone's about to beat you, to know how to empathically connect with what's alive in that person. We teach police how to do this in dangerous conditions. A lot of research has been documented that police are far more likely to come out alive when dealing with violent people armed with empathy than a gun. But, to ask kids to do it is a bigger challenge, and so we've got to give the children a lot of practice.

If you're around parents who think that parents always know what's right, and if the other person's wrong they should be punished for it, then you're likely to beat your own child. Until we can get ahold of the parents the child lives with, we teach the children the best self defense we know: empathic connection.

Dealing with Your Own Angry Behavior

UM: How do you deal with your own personal nonviolent behavior when you've communicated with another person, gone through everything, and you get to the point where you feel like blowing up? When the traffic's bad, when you're going to the airport, or whatever . . .

MBR: If you follow me around when I leave here this evening, you will probably see twenty such situations between now and when I get to Santa Barbara tonight. My partner's sleeping now or she would verify that.

UM: And you've gone through that whole process of the mentally calming yourself down and doing all that . . .

MBR: Yes. So I suffer now for about thirty seconds instead of about three hours. But, I still get triggered. You see, there is this horrible breed of violent, evil people called "people who don't move fast enough." When I want to get through the ticket line, and I want to sit down and just relax, this breed of people, these jerks are all over the damn planet and they're placed here to aggravate the hell out of me. There's an international plot to test out my patience in my Nonviolent Communication . . .

UM: So, do you have a trick or a special trigger that you've come up with? Do you "count to ten," or . . .

MBR: No, my anger is valuable. It's really a blessing. When I'm angry I know I need to slow down, look at what I'm telling myself. Translate the judgments that are making me angry and get in touch with my needs.

UM: So, you believe anger is justified in certain situations?

MBR: Anger is always justified in the sense that it's the inevitable result of life-alienated, violence provocative thinking. Anger is not the problem. It's the thinking that's going on in us when we're angry that's the problem.

UM: And what is the process that you use to deal with it?

MBR: I slow down and I enjoy the judgement show going on in my head. I don't tell myself I "shouldn't" think that way. That's perpetuating it. I don't say it's wrong. I don't say what my son once said to me, when I said these judgmental thoughts out loud: "You go around the world teaching communication?" I try not to say that to myself . . . I don't think, "It's justified." I just see it, connect with the need behind it, and give empathy to myself. I hear the need behind this moralistic thinking.

As an example, I might be frustrated because I'd like the line to go faster, but in the ten minutes that I'm going to be in that line, I'm not going to be putting additional stress on my heart. (By the way, research in the medical arena shows a high correlation between "Type A" thinking, which is what I call moralistic or judgmental thinking, and heart disease.) So, I'd like to slow down the stress on my heart to about thirty beats-a-second, rather than for ten minutes being in that line angry at this person up front who's taken up all this time talking to the ticket seller. Don't they know I'm back here? I can eat my heart, or I can choose to really transform that frustration. What could I do in these ten minutes? Carry something to read in the line.

UM: Is the ultimate goal to not be perturbed by it at all? Is that where you see yourself eventually?

MBR: The ultimate goal is to spend as many of my moments in life as I can in that world that the poet Rumi talks about, "a place beyond rightness and wrongness."

Learning to Deal with a Difficult Person

UM: Aside from right and wrong, I think we all have our conditioning, a certain chemistry and openness towards some people and not toward others, based on our upbringing, personal habits and all. And I often don't know how to genuinely feel open, warm to people who are different, really different than I am. And I'm not necessarily just talking about racism. It might just be people with different habits, different ways to go about things, and so I'm confused about how to genuinely develop more tolerance. And it's more difficult in this politically correct society that says we should be tolerant.

MBR: First, by getting the word "should" out of there. As long as I think I "should" do it, I'll resist it, even if I want very much to do it. Hearing "should" from inside or outside takes all the joy out of doing it. I try to never do anything I should do, but follow Joseph Campbell's suggestion. After studying comparative religion and mythology for forty-three years, Campbell said, "You know, after all of my research, it's amazing that all religions are saying the same thing: Don't do anything that isn't playful."

Don't do anything that isn't play. He says it another way: "Follow your bliss," come from this energy of how to make the world fun and learnable.

MBR: Let's talk for a minute about "tolerance." There are a lot of people that I can't stand being around. And they are my best gurus. They teach me about what's going on in me that makes it hard to see the divine energy in them. I want to learn from anything that keeps me from connecting to that energy. Fortunately, there are a lot of people I can't stand; I have a lot of learning opportunities. I practice. I ask, "What does this person do that is a trigger for my judging them?" First I try to get clear about what they do, and second, conscious about how I'm judging that person who makes me so angry. The third step is to look behind my judgment to see what particular need of mine is not getting met in relation to that person. I try to give myself empathy for what need of mine isn't met in relation to that person. Fourth, I say to myself, "When the person does that thing that I don't like, what personal need are they trying to meet?" I try to empathize with what's alive in them when they do it.

These people that I can't stand are my best teachers of Nonviolent Communication if I do that exercise with them.

Anger towards Mother Role-Play

UM: I would like to know if you would be willing to help me with some healing with my mother? I'm going to be visiting her for Thanksgiving.

MBR: Let's do it. I'll be your mother, and you play yourself. (BEGINS ROLE PLAY) Well, son, I've got my empathy ears on now and I would like very much to hear anything that's alive in you that makes it less-than-totally enjoyable for you to be around me.

UM: Where do I begin?

MBR: Oh, good, there's a lot I can learn.

UM: I'm so frustrated and angry and discouraged, and I feel despair around how negative you are, how you're always looking at things to criticize about the world, about me, about life, about the government. I'm angry that you painted this picture that the world is a horrible place and then said it to me and to my sisters.

MBR: Let me see if I can get that. I hear two important messages in there that I don't want to miss. First is, if I'm hearing you correctly, you'd like some understanding about how painful it is for you to be around me when I'm in so much pain . . . and how it leaves you constantly feeling under some pressure to have to some way deal with my pain.

UM: Yes.

MBR: And then the second thing that I'm hearing that you'd like from me is some understanding of how much pain you carry with you from having been exposed to this for so long, that you'd like to not have so much pain in how you see things.

UM: That's partly accurate. I'm angry because it feels like I have to fight inside of myself, to protect my own ability to choose, to perceive things the way I want.

MBR: So, how wonderful it would be if you didn't have to work so hard to live in a world that is quite different than the one that I painted for you.

UM: Yeah.

MBR: Yeah. How much you'd like to live in that other world and how sad it is to see how much of your energy goes into the one that I helped you learn to live in.

UM: Yeah, and this sounds blaming—and it is—but that's where I'm at right now.

MBR: I can't hear blame, son. I have my NVC ears on. All I can hear is beauty.

UM: I'm angry that you're just in so much pain that that's all you present, and that you didn't say, "I'm in a lot of pain, but you don't have to be." And I'm angry that I wasn't given any encouragement to choose a different way of looking at the world, and when I do present a different way, you feel threatened and you try to devalue and diminish what I perceive.

MBR: I want to reflect that, check with you to see whether it could have at least made things more bearable for you, while I was in this pain, if I could've said, "Hey, this is just how I look at it and I'm not encouraging you to see it this way." But I presented it in a way that sounded like this is the way the world is, and as a child you internalized that. And that is now what makes it so hard for you to live in the world of your choosing, rather than the one I painted for you.

UM: Yes. And I go into that child place a lot when I'm with you. I don't have the distance that I feel like I need to be able to say, "Ah, that's just my mom and . . ."

MBR: Yeah.

UM: It still feels like it threatens my autonomy to hear your feelings.

MBR: Yeah, you hear those feelings and you lose connection with the world you want to be in and go into this world that I painted for you.

UM: Yeah. And I'm worried because I'm going to visit you on Thanksgiving and I know a lot of the strategies that I've used in the past are still alive in me, like nodding my head up and down, pretending to listen when I'm really angry, and I've left my body, and I'm too scared to express my real feelings, and I'm worried that I'm going to do that again.

MBR: Yeah.

UM: And I'm worried that if I do try to be authentic with you that I'm going to be criticized for having these feelings.

MBR: You hate to be in this situation where the only two options you can imagine are hiding yourself or trying to be honest and making a bigger mess. You'd really like there to be some other connection between us beside that.

UM: Yeah. And I'm worried about the part of me that is so hurt about this that I want to shame you and make you wrong.

MBR: It's so strong in you how you suffered that you need this understanding desperately for how much you've paid for this.

UM: Yeah. Yeah. The thing that scares me the most though, is not being authentic and making a mess, because I have some training in being able to clean it up. What I hate about myself is that I can freeze up and just not be there.

MBR: Yeah.

UM: And not take care of myself, and not speak up, and I'm worried about that tendency.

MBR: So as uncomfortable as it is for you to imagine speaking up and having to clean up the mess, that's less toxic for you than continuing to hide yourself and not express yourself—as scary as it is to do that.

UM: I have a lot of pain about internalizing the labels "too sensitive," and "hypersensitive," the labels that you use to express your being overwhelmed when you hear my feelings.

MBR: Yeah, yeah, yeah. You wish you could hear through that and hear my pain without hearing any criticism, but it's a real strain for you to do that.

UM: Yeah.

MBR: Is there more you'd like me to hear before I respond?

UM: I'm really worried about how much pain is still alive in me, and how that comes out as me wanting to make you wrong, wanting to shame you and beat you up for what I perceive you did to me.

MBR: Yeah, the pain is so strong in you, and you need to get it out, but you're afraid that the only way it might come out is going to be interpreted by me in a way that will make both of us even more distant from each other. And that's not what you want. But you do want to be able to get that pain out and dealt with.

UM: Yeah, I'm worried about intellectualizing, and I wish I had the permission, the psychic permission to just scream and stamp my feet and not say any words and have that heard, because we get into our heads, and I hate that.

MBR: Yeah. So, you want to be sure that if we do use words, that they really connect us to life and not take us further from it. And at the moment it's hard to imagine any words that would do that. It seems like to get all the pain out you just have to scream or stomp or something.

UM: And I'm also connected to a part of me that just wants to come home and get the nurturing that I have not gotten as a child in this family, and I'm worried that that's not a very realistic need to try to get met in this family.

MBR: So, there's more than just resolving all this pain. You really have a dream of a nurturing relationship, of feeling you're valued, of enjoying our being with each other. That seems so far off given all the pain that you're going through, that it's hard to even imagine we could get to that stage of really being nurturing for one another.

UM: Uh huh. To be honest, it's hard to imagine you ever giving that, because you're so caught up in your own suffering.

MBR: Yeah. So hard to even imagine. Anything more you want me to hear before I respond?

UM: You know, if you talk about how much you hate the president, even if I agree with you, I don't want to hear it, and I'd rather punch you in the face.

MBR: So, whatever I'm talking about, whether it's the president or something else, as soon as you see me in pain, you then get yourself in such pain, that it's not a place you want to continue to be in.

UM: I don't have any idea why, intellectually, but just hearing you vent your judgments about people pisses me off: I don't want to be a sounding board for your story telling. If I saw you releasing your pain and getting empathy for that, it would be a different story, but . . .

MBR: You're fed up with feeling that somehow you have to heal that pain, and not knowing how to do it, and getting yourself down. You want something else out of any relationship you're in, besides being in that role.

UM: Yeah.

MBR: Having to listen to it, and then somehow, make me feel better.

UM: Uh huh. I wish I could find a way to enjoy it. You know, hearing your judgments versus the way I hear a friend's judgments: You and I sometimes have a party hurting each other . . . And I'm not there, because I have this critical voice inside telling me it's my responsibility.

MBR: You're aware that part of the issue is telling yourself that somehow you need to fix me, your Mom. But, also, you want me to see that there are things that I say and do that provoke that.

UM: Yeah, it would feel really nice for me if you said, "You know, I've got some pain and I'd like to vent: Can I have an ear?" To actually ask for permission. Then I could get my needs met for respect.

MBR: Yeah. I'd like to respond now. Can you hear me, or would you like me to hear more of you?

UM: I can say a lot more, but I feel okay about hearing you now.

MBR: Well, I'm so relieved that you haven't given up on our relationship, that you still are working to try to find a way to make it not only bearable, but nurturing. And I'm sure you've been close to giving up on it. I can't tell you what a gift it is, that in spite of the pain that you're telling me about, that you're still looking for a hope, some glimmer that we can learn to nurture each other.

UM: I don't know that I have that hope, but I know that if I work on this a little bit, I'll have better relationships with women.

MBR: So, even if you can't imagine getting nurture from me, you would hope at least that you could with other women. There's so much I want to tell you that's stimulated in me by what you've said, but at the moment, there's just a horrible sadness to see that I handled my pain in a way that didn't meet one of the needs that I've had my whole life, the strongest need that I can think of: to nurture you. And to see that instead of nurturing you in a way that I would've liked, I've been a stimulus for so much pain for you. It's enormously frightening to look at my depth of sadness about that. It's one thing that I had to suffer myself, but oh my god, to have contributed to all this pain in you. That's a real, real painful sadness to look at. And I'd like to know how you feel when you hear me say that.

UM: I feel kind of numb. I think I'm protecting myself.

MBR: That's what I was afraid of, that even now you feel that you have to do something about it. I really do want you to know that with these ears on all I want is empathy. Nothing else. And if you can't give it, I can hear that without hearing it as a rejection or creating more pain. So, I can hear that you're kind of numb and part of you wants to resonate to it, but part of you is afraid of getting into the old now-you-have-to-do-something-about-it.

Now, I'd like to tell you what goes on in me when I've been doing that over the years. When I hear how you would've liked for me to have said it, really I want to cry because it makes me aware that I would've liked to have said it in that way. Then I ask myself what kept me from doing it, and that's when I want to cry. I can't even imagine that anyone really cares about what's going on for me. And then what you said helped me to realize that I've been asking for it in a way that leads to self-fulfilling prophecies. The way I've been asking for it, how can anybody enjoy giving it to me? And I just felt such a depth of sadness that I didn't know other ways of saying, "Hey, I'm in pain and I need some attention."

I don't want you to take responsibility for it. I just need somehow to feel that somebody cares about what's going on for me. The only way I knew to ask for that provoked just the opposite from almost everybody, going back to the time I was a child. I never had the feeling that my needs mattered to somebody. Therefore, to ask for it in a way the other person might enjoy hearing it wasn't a possibility. I just get desperate and express it in the only way I know how: out of desperation. And then I see how it affects other people, and I get even more desperate. I'd like to know how you feel when I tell you that.

UM: Sad, but somewhat relieved to be able to hear some of what was behind the urgency of your expression. Some relief in just connecting with it.

MBR: I'm feeling very vulnerable about our revelation of ourselves. How would you feel if I asked the group for their reaction to what we've been saying?

UM: I'd probably enjoy that.

MBR: Okay, does anybody have any feelings, reactions to our dialogue?

Reactions to the Role-Play

UF: Somehow, it just makes my heart smile to see men being so responsive to each other in such a compassionate way. This is a new kind of experience for me.

MBR: We're not *real* men. (said jokingly)

UF: Your modeling it for me opens up a possibility for a way for men to act. So, I'm grateful.

UM: I, too, am grateful. It really touched my heart deeply, because my mother and I have a similar dynamic, one that I've not found an effective way to deal with. I've just kind of gone to a place of hopelessness about it. And as I was listening to Marshall mourn in the mother role, with the sadness over how her intention was for her son to be happy, and how important that was to her, I felt some healing for me, knowing that's what's important to my mother—that it was never her intention to make my life hard. It was healing for me to hear what she may have been going through and to hear your dialogue. I really appreciate that.

UM: Well, I feel very grateful for the experience, because I could really sense the humanity behind the words. I don't know if anybody's heard about "vibrations," but I felt something at one point that took away the separateness between me and each one in this room. I felt really connected. And on the other side, I'm a little sad, because I really would like to see people—myself included—happy, you know. And I'm realizing what you were saying when you were role-playing the mother: That there is something that blocks the humanity in each one of us, and it's amazing how quick a solution can happen once one or maybe both persons are able to open up. I think the technique helps a lot, but it's also about your ability to connect with your heart; it's about the presence I felt. Like believing in God. I think that's a good description of what I felt in the moment. Thank you very much.

UM (from role play): What's alive in me is my sadness, identifying with you, recognizing that I've given up on healing my relationship with my own mother . . . how I was just going to heal my relationship with women without having to heal with my mother. And how I don't know how to approach her, or even if I can or should, because I don't think she could really respond like that to me.

MBR: How do you think she would respond about hearing this recording?

UM: I don't know. It has been healing for me; maybe it would heal her or something.

MBR: I'd like you to try it, and if it works beautifully, I'd like you to call me up and tell me. And if it messes things up, call my staff.

UM: I feel some hope after hearing that: not that I could stay with feelings and needs the whole time by any means, but I just feel some hope. Even if I screw it up, there's some hope and energy to try with my own brother, the same kind of thing. Thank you.

Marshall's Mother's Gift to Him

MBR: I'd like to share with you a gift I got. I had very similar pain in relationship to my mother, and you were speaking like it was me. And I want to tell you about some major surgery that I had that helped me get out of it, not surgery done on me, but that my mother had at a workshop of mine that she came to.

In the workshop, women in the group were talking about how scary it was for them as women to express needs directly, and how much their personal relationships with men were getting all mucked up because of it. The only way they knew how to express needs got the opposite of what they wanted. Then they got more bitter, which made it worse.

Well, one woman after another was saying how hard it was for her to say her need. My mother gets up and leaves, goes to the bathroom. And I'm starting to worry because she really was in there a long time. And when she comes out I notice how pale she is and I ask, "Mother, are you all right?" She says, "Now I am."

"It was very upsetting for me to hear the discussion, because when I heard the women talking about how hard it was for them to express their needs, it had reminded me of something." I said, "Do you mind telling me what it was, Mother?"

She told me this story. "When I was fourteen, my sister, your aunt Minnie, had her appendix taken out, and then your aunt Alice bought her a little purse. How I cherished that purse, what I wouldn't have given for that purse, but in our family you never ask for what you want or need. You would hear back from one of the older kids, 'You know how poor we are. Why are you asking for what you need?' But I wanted it so badly that I started to complain of pains in my side. They took me to two doctors who couldn't find anything, but the third one said maybe we should do exploratory surgery."

They took out my mother's appendix. And it worked: My aunt Alice bought her a purse just like the one that she wanted but couldn't ask for. But that wasn't the end of it. Mother told me, "And then I was lying in bed in the hospital in a lot of pain from the operation, but so happy. The nurse came in and stuck a thermometer in my mouth, then went out and another nurse came in. I wanted her to see my purse but I could only say 'Mmmm, mmmm, mmmm' because of the thing in my mouth. The nurse said, 'For me? Thank you,' and she took the purse. And I couldn't ask for it back."

That was such a gift that my mother gave me, because just seeing how hard it was for her to express her needs, what she would go through, helped me see everything I hated her for. I understand about when she asked for the things that just aggravated the hell out of me, there was desperation behind it. I could see why she couldn't just come out and say it. So, that major surgery helped shake me out of that, see her pain as a "Damn-it . . ." That really helped.

UF (to role-play participant): I wanted to tell you how much I appreciated your willingness to be vulnerable and to express all of your anger and your hurt and your pain. And you may be surprised that your mother may be so willing, so anxious to open that up. I'm going to buy the audiotape and take it to my son.

UM: Could you say a few things that would bring some closure to my dialogue with you? I'm thinking about getting the audiotape and playing it for my mother when I visit her, and this brings up a lot of fear. What I'm telling myself is, we said some pretty strong, harsh things and, while I don't have any hope that I can have a better relationship with my mom, I'm worried that she might not be able to hear that as me venting in the moment.

MBR: That's the danger, but if she stays with it long enough and sees how I heard the beauty behind it, she'll also be learning Nonviolent Communication.

UM: I just realized I can tell her before putting on the tape some of the things I said I was saying just for the purpose of expressing the really strong emotion in the moment: She understands that very well. She taught me that.

MBR: And then you can say, "And Mother, I'd like you to see how Marshall handled it in your role. And I'd like you to tell me afterwards how you felt about how he played your role. How he dealt with it when I called him these names."

UM: I'm worried she might want you for a son.

UF: I want Marshall for a mother.

Summary

There are **THREE PRIMARY STEPS** in creating a bridge of empathy between people seeking healing or reconciliation in a significant relationship.

STEP ONE IS for someone to listen empathically to a person who is hurting, angry, or frightened. The listener is present for the person, listening for "what is alive in them" without judgments, moralizing, diagnosing, or offering unsolicited advice. We learned the difference between "empathizing"—that full presence with the other that is empty of attention on our own feelings—and "sympathizing" which says, "I know what you're feeling" and is self-reflective, causing our attention to leave the one we are listening to.

Every effort is made to give the hurting person all the empathic attention that they need, until they experience some relief. We check in as often as we need to be sure we are following and understanding. We may check in silently, or out loud, asking questions to be sure we understand. When the other person feels satisfied, the listener can move on.

STEP TWO in healing or reconciliaton NVC style is the "post-empathic request," in which the listener helps find out what else the person needs right now. Getting in touch with unmet needs is important to the healing process, as is making requests to the receiver about what would meet those needs now, in the present moment.

We saw that there are three ways to bring into play the role of the "other party" in a conflict. The first way is to act as a third party. The second way is to play the role of that other person in the conflict, and the third is to get that actual person to participate in the dialogue.

After the person has fully expressed their pain, discovered their present needs in the situation, and identified requests that would meet those needs, they may then be able to hear the feelings, needs, and requests of the listener.

STEP THREE has the listener now share what she is feeling about what she's just heard. The listener mourns by recognizing the part she's played in creating the situation and gets in touch with what needs of her own were unmet through the speaker's actions, and with the pain stimulated in the other. She also identifies the actions she wishes they had taken instead. This mourning process is different from an apology, which implies blame or wrong-doing. The mourner acknowledges what they would rather have done that would have met everyone's needs more fully. This allows deep hurt, sadness, or remorse to arise and be heard by the person we hurt. The mourner may request to be listened to silently while their feelings are expressed, or may ask for feedback afterwards.

If both parties wish, they may trade roles and repeat the empathy and mourning steps in order to allow a fuller understanding between them about their situation. If afterwards they still need more help, they may request the services of a "third-sider," someone trained in the use of Nonviolent Communication who will mediate the healing and reconciliation process.

Some Basic Feelings We All Have

Feelings when needs "are" fulfilled

- Amazed
- Confident
- Energetic
- Glad
- Inspired
- Joyous
- Optimistic
- Relieved
- Surprised
- Touched
- Comfortable
- Eager
- Fulfilled
- Hopeful
- Intrigued
- Moved
- Proud
- Stimulated
- Thankful
- Trustful

Feelings when needs "are not" fulfilled

- Angry
- Confused
- Disappointed
- Distressed
- Frustrated
- Hopeless
- Irritated
- Nervous
- Puzzled
- Sad
- Annoyed
- Concerned
- Discouraged
- Embarrassed
- Helpless
- Impatient
- Lonely
- Overwhelmed
- Reluctant
- Uncomfortable

Some Basic Needs We All Have

Autonomy
- Choosing dreams/goals/values
- Choosing plans for fulfilling one's dreams, goals, values

Celebration
- Celebrate the creation of life and dreams fulfilled
- Celebrate losses: loved ones, dreams, etc. (mourning)

Integrity
- Authenticity • Creativity
- Meaning • Self-worth

Interdependence
- Acceptance • Appreciation
- Closeness • Community
- Consideration
- Contribute to the enrichment of life
- Emotional Safety • Empathy

Physical Nurturance
- Air • Food
- Movement, exercise
- Protection from life-threatening forms of life: viruses, bacteria, insects, predatory animals
- Rest • Sexual expression
- Shelter • Touch • Water

Play
- Fun • Laughter

Spiritual Communion
- Beauty • Harmony
- Inspiration • Order • Peace

- Honesty (the empowering honesty that enables us to learn from our limitations)
- Love • Reassurance
- Respect • Support
- Trust • Understanding

About CNVC and NVC

2428 Foothill Blvd., Suite E, La Crescenta, CA 91214
Tel: (818) 957-9393 • Fax: (818) 957-1424
Email: cnvc@cnvc.org • Website: www.cnvc.org

The **Center for Nonviolent Communication** is a global organization whose vision is a world where everyone's needs are met peacefully. Our mission is to contribute to this vision by facilitating the creation of life-enriching systems within ourselves, inter-personally, and within organizations. We do this by living and teaching the process of Nonviolent Communication[SM] (NVC), which strengthens people's ability to compassionately connect with themselves and one another, share resources, and resolve conflicts peacefully.

CNVC is dedicated to fostering a compassionate response to people by honoring our universally shared needs for autonomy, celebration, integrity, interdependence, physical nurturance, play, and spiritual communion. We are committed to functioning, at every level of our organization and in all of our interactions, in harmony with the process we teach, operating by consensus, using NVC to resolve conflicts, and providing NVC training for our staff. We often work collaboratively with other organizations for a peaceful, just and ecologically balanced world.

Purpose, Mission, History, and Projects

For many years the Center for Nonviolent Communication has been showing people how to connect in ways that inspire compassionate results. We are now seeking funds to support projects in North America, Latin America, South America, Europe, Africa, South Asia, Brazil, and the Middle East, and to support our innovative projects for educators, parents, social change, and prison work.

A list of CNVC certified trainers and contact information for them may be found on the Center's website. This list is updated monthly. The website also includes information about CNVC sponsored trainings and links to affiliated regional websites. CNVC invites you to consider bringing NVC training to your business, school, church, or community group. For current information about trainings scheduled in your area, or if you would like to organize NVC trainings, be on the CNVC mailing list or support our efforts to create a more peaceful world, please contact CNVC.

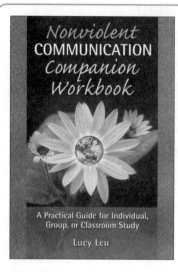

Nonviolent Communication℠ Companion Workbook

by Lucy Leu

ISBN: 1-892005-04-2
Price: $19.95 US • Trade Paper 7x10
Distributed by IPG: 800-888-4741

Create your life, your relationships, and your world in harmony with your values.

It's time to put Nonviolent Communication into practice, and this workbook will help you do it. Supporting you through each chapter of Rosenberg's book, this workbook contains refreshing and empowering ideas for: dealing with anger, resolving conflict, improving internal dialogue, and relating more compassionately with others.

- For **INDIVIDUALS**, this workbook provides you with activities and ideas for employing the liberating principles of NVC in your daily life.

- For **GROUP PRACTICE**, this workbook offers guidance for getting started, curriculum, and activities for each chapter.

- For **TEACHERS**, this workbook serves as the basis for developing your own courses, or to augment an existing curriculum.

LUCY LEU is the former Board President of the Center for Nonviolent Communication, and editor of the best selling *Nonviolent Communication: A Language of Life*. Currently she heads the Freedom Project, bringing NVC training to prison inmates to contribute to their reintegration into society. For information about the Freedom Project email: freedom_project@hotmail.com

Available from CNVC, all major bookstores and Amazon.com
Distributed by IPG: 800-888-4741

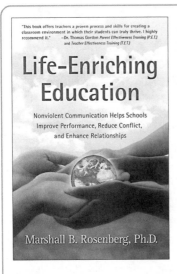

"This book offers teachers a proven process and skills for creating a classroom environment in which their students can truly thrive. I highly recommend it." —Dr. Thomas Gordon *Parent Effectiveness Training (P.E.T.)* and *Teacher Effectiveness Training (T.E.T.)*

Life-Enriching Education

Nonviolent Communication Helps Schools Improve Performance, Reduce Conflict, and Enhance Relationships

Marshall B. Rosenberg, Ph.D.

Life-Enriching Education

by Marshall B. Rosenberg, Ph.D.

ISBN: 1-892005-05-0
Trade Paper 6x9 • Price: $12.95 US
Distributed by IPG: 800-888-4741

*When Students Love to Learn
and Teachers Love to Teach . . .*

Today many schools struggle with low achievement, disrespect among students and teachers, and safety issues as their primary concerns. Students and their families are unhappy, teachers and administrators are frustrated, and everyone can't wait for the weekend.

What's needed is a new approach to education, one that serves the lives of everyone in the learning community. Marshall Rosenberg realizes this vision in Life-Enriching Education. You'll discover an approach to education based on mutually respectful relationships between students, teachers, administrators, and parents.

You'll learn practical skills that show you how to:

• Increase student interest, achievement, and retention
• Create a safe and supportive learning and working atmosphere
• Cultivate emotional intelligence, respect, and compassion
• Resolve conflicts and prevent or de-escalate violence
• Re-discover the joy of teaching motivated students

"This book offers teachers a proven process, and skills for creating a classroom environment in which their students can truly thrive. I highly recommend it."

—Dr. Thomas Gordon Author, *Parent Effectiveness Training* (P.E.T.) and *Teacher Effectiveness Training* (T.E.T.)

**Available from CNVC, all major bookstores and Amazon.com
Distributed by IPG: 800-888-4741**

Additional NVC Books from PuddleDancer Press

We Can Work It Out $5.95
Resolving Conflicts Peacefully and Powerfully   (6x9, 32 pages)
by Marshall B. Rosenberg, Ph.D. • Practical suggestions for fostering
caring, genuine cooperation, and satisfying resolutions in even the most difficult
situations. ISBN: 1-892005-12-3

Raising Children Compassionately $5.95
Parenting the Nonviolent Communication Way   (6x9, 32 pages)
by Marshall B. Rosenberg, Ph.D. • This booklet, filled with insights
and stories, will prove invaluable for parents, teachers and others who want
to nurture children and also themselves. ISBN: 1-892005-09-3

Teaching Children Compassionately $7.95
How Students and Teachers Can Succeed with Mutual   (6x9, 48 pages)
Understanding • by Marshall B. Rosenberg, Ph.D.
Skills for creating a successful classroom—from a keynote address and workshop
given to a national conference of Montessori educators. ISBN: 1-892005-11-5

What's Making You Angry? $5.95
10 Steps to Transforming Anger So Everyone Wins   (6x9, 32 pages)
by Shari Klein and Neill Gibson • A step-by-step guide to re-focus your
attention when you're angry, and create outcomes that are satisfying for everyone.
ISBN: 1-892005-13-1

The Heart of Social Change $7.95
How to Make a Difference in Your World   (6x9, 48 pages)
by Marshall B. Rosenberg, Ph.D. • Marshall offers an insightful
perspective on effective social change, and how-to examples. ISBN: 1-892005-10-7

Parenting From Your Heart $7.95
Sharing the Gifts of Compassion, Connection, and Choice   (6x9, 48 pages)
by Inbal Kashtan • Addresses the challenges of parenting with real-world solutions
for creating family relationships that meet everyone's needs. ISBN: 1-892005-08-5

Getting Past the Pain Between Us $7.95
Healing and Reconciliation Without Compromise   (6x9, 48 pages)
by Marshall B. Rosenberg, Ph.D. • Learn the healing power of listening
and speaking from the heart. Skills for resolving conflicts, healing old hurts, and
reconciling strained relationships. ISBN: 1-892005-07-7

Available from CNVC, all major bookstores and Amazon.com. Distributed by IPG: 800-888-4741
For more information about these booklets visit www.NonviolentCommunication.com

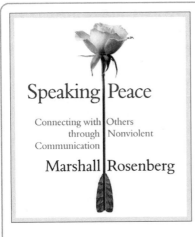

NONVIOLENT COMMUNICATION MATERIALS
Available from CNVC at www.CNVC.org or call 800-255-7696

The Compassionate Classroom $18
Relationship Based Teaching and Learning   (7.5x9, 187 pages)
by Sura Hart and Victoria Kindle Hodson, M.A. • This new book provides
an overview of the NVC process and its relationship to successful teaching and learning,
and specific examples of how NVC can be used in elementary school classrooms includes
playful exercises, lesson plans, and skill-building activities and games.

The Giraffe Classroom $18
by Nancy Sokol Green • Humorous, creative, and   (8.5x11, spiral bound, 122 pages)
thought provoking activities. Ideal for teachers, parents, and anyone who wants to use
concrete exercises to learn the process of NVC.

The Mayor of Jackal Heights $10
by Rita Herzog and Kathy Smith • A boy mayor   (8.5x11, spiral bound, 122 pages)
begins to learn how to tame his town full of jackals with the help of his wise friend,
Giraffe. A beautifully illustrated story for children of all ages.

A Model for Nonviolent Communication $8
by Marshall B. Rosenberg • A handbook describing the basics   (5.5x8.5, 56 pages)
of Nonviolent Communication, including exercises to help readers check their
understanding of the process. Updated, expanded, and revised.

Duck Tales and Jackal Taming Hints $4
by Marshall B. Rosenberg, Ph.D. • A whimsical tale about skills   (7x9, 28 pages)
needed to understand human beings, even when their communication makes them
sound like deranged jackals.

Communication Basics $4
An Overview of Nonviolent Communication   (24 pages)
by Rachelle Lamb • This new booklet provides a clear, concise, and handy summary
of what one might learn in an introductory training in Nonviolent Communication.

The Spiritual Basis of Nonviolent Communication $2
A Question and Answer Session with   (8.5x11, 8 pages)
Marshall Rosenberg, Ph.D. • Las Bases Espirituales De La Communicacion No
Violenta—Spanish language version available at same price.

Audiotapes, CDs, and Videotapes

Introduction To A Model for Nonviolent Communication $10
by Marshall B. Rosenberg, Ph.D. • Marshall Rosenberg introduces   (Audio, 90 min.)
a model for Nonviolent Communication through discussion, stories, and music.

Connecting Compassionately $10
by Marshall B. Rosenberg, Ph.D. • Workshop presentation by   (Audio, 90 min.)
Marshall Rosenberg explains the NVC process for dealing with frustrations and blocks
in communications.

Connecting Compassionately $10
by Marshall B. Rosenberg, Ph.D. • Workshop presentation by   (Audio, 90 min.)
Marshall Rosenberg explains the NVC process for dealing with frustrations and blocks
in communications.

Expressing and Receiving Anger $10
by Marshall B. Rosenberg, Ph.D. • How to use the principles of   (Audio, 90 min.)
Nonviolent Communication to fully express and receive anger.

Nonviolent Communication for Educators $10
by Marshall B. Rosenberg, Ph.D. • Keynote address to the   (Audio, 90 min.)
National Conference of Montessori Educators—will be of special interest to teachers,
parents and anyone who works with children.

A Heart to Heart Talk • by Marshall B. Rosenberg, Ph.D. $10
Workshop presentation at the National Conference of Montessori Educators, (Audio, 90 min.)
offers an in-depth exploration of Nonviolent Communication in the field of education.

Speaking Peace • by Marshall B. Rosenberg, Ph.D. . . . . 2 CD set: $25
This recording, produced by Sounds True, explains the purpose . . . . . . 2 Audio set: $20
of NVC, how to use the 4 components of the NVC model to express ourselves   (2.5 hrs.)
honestly and respond empathically to others, and to bring about change within
ourselves, others, and within larger social systems; includes songs, stories and examples.

The Basics of Nonviolent Communication $50
An Introductory Training   (2 videotapes, 3 hrs)
by Marshall B. Rosenberg, Ph.D. • This edited one-day training shows how we
can connect with others in a way that enables everyone's needs to be met through
natural giving.

Making Life Wonderful $145
An Intermediate Training   (4 videotapes, over 8 hours)
by Marshall B. Rosenberg, Ph.D. • Improve relationships with self and others
by increasing fluency in NVC. Two-day training session in San Francisco filled with
insights, examples, extended role-plays, stories, and songs that will deepen your
grasp of NVC.

ORDERING FROM CNVC:
(10% Member Discount available—Prices may change.)

Mail: CNVC, 2428 Foothill Blvd., Suite E, La Crescenta, CA 91214

Phone: 800-255-7696 (toll free order line) or by Fax: 1-818-957-1424

Shipping: First item $5.00, each additional $1.00 (For orders shipped outside
the United States, call 1-818-957-9393 to determine actual shipping charges.
Please pay with US dollars only.

Contributions And Membership: A contribution of $35 or more qualifies you
as a member of CNVC and entitles you to a 10% discount on CNVC materials
ordered from the Center. Your tax-deductible contribution of any amount will
be gratefully received and will help support CNVC projects worldwide.

About The Author

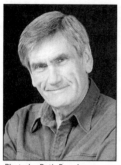

MARSHALL B. ROSENBERG, PH.D. is Founder and Director of Educational Services for the Center for Nonviolent Communication (CNVC).

Growing up in a turbulent Detroit neighborhood, Dr. Rosenberg developed a keen interest in new forms of communication that would provide peaceful alternatives to the violence he encountered. His interest led to a Ph.D. in clinical psychology from the University of Wisconsin in 1961. His subsequent life experience and study of comparative religion motivated him to develop Nonviolent Communication (NVC).

Dr. Rosenberg first used NVC in federally funded projects to provide mediation and communication skills training during the 1960s. He founded the Center for Nonviolent Communication (CNVC) in 1984. Since then CNVC has grown into an international nonprofit organization with over 100 trainers. They provide training in 30 countries in North and South America, Europe, Asia, the Middle East, and Africa, and offer workshops for educators, counselors, parents, health care providers, mediators, business managers, prison inmates and guards, police, military personnel, clergy, and government officials.

Dr. Rosenberg has initiated peace programs in war torn areas including Rwanda, Burundi, Nigeria, Malaysia, Indonesia, Sri Lanka, Sierra Leone, the Middle East, Colombia, Serbia, Croatia, and Northern Ireland. Funded by UNESCO, the CNVC team in Yugoslavia has trained tens of thousands of students and teachers. The government of Israel has officially recognized NVC and is now offering training in hundreds of schools in that country.

Dr. Rosenberg is currently based in Wasserfallenhof, Switzerland, and travels regularly offering NVC training and conflict mediation.